"وَّخَلَقْنٰكُمْ اَزْوَاجًا"

Etiquette
Of
Intimacy
In
Islam

Ibn-e-Anees

2024

Copyright ©

Table of Contents

BEG FOR PARDON.................................7

ABOUT THE BOOK.............................9

PREFACE 11

KINDNESS TO WIFE 16

PRAYING FOR THE WIFE....................17

PERFORM SALAT WITH WIFE 18

DUA OF INTIMATE 21

HOW TO HAVE INTERCOURSE? 21

FORBIDDEN IN THE ANUS.....................24

WHEN INTERCOURSE AGAIN, PERFORM ABLUTION 27

TAKING A JOINT SHOWER WITH THE SPOUSE28

INTERCOURSE WITH A MENSTRUATING WOMAN IS PROHIBITED.................................30

ATONEMENT FOR THE ONE WHO HAS SEXUAL INTERCOURSE WHILE MENSTRUATING 32

HOW MUCH BENEFIT CAN BE TAKEN FROM A MENSTRUATING WOMAN?.........................33

HOW LONG AFTER A WOMAN IS PURIFIED IS IT ACCEPTABLE TO HAVE SEX WITH HER? 34

AZAL LEGAL OR ILLEGAL? 35

WHAT IS THE INTENTION OF A HUSBAND AND WIFE IN MARRIAGE? 37

SPOUSES SHOULD NOT SHARE THEIR SECRETS WITH OTHERS.....................40

SHARIAH PROCEDURE OF MARRIAGE 41

DRUMMING, SINGING, FIREWORKS, AND MIXED GATHERINGS ON THE OCCASION OF MARRIAGE. 42

Playing Drums, Playing Songs Is Forbidden In Shariat. 42

Fireworks, Air Firing. 44

Mixed Gathering. 45

NONE MUSLIM MARRIAGE RITUALS 46

PLACING THE QUR'AN ON THE BRIDE'S HEAD AT THE TIME OF MARRIAGE.....................47

WALIMA SUNNAH OR WAJIB? 48

When Is Walima Sunnah After Three Days Or After One Day? 48

Walima Is Permissible Even Without Meat. 49

Forbidden To Invite Only Rich People To Walima.. 50

AVOID AFFAIRS AGAINST SHARIAT 51

Plucking Of Eyebrow Hair Etc. 51

Longer Nails And Nail Polish. 52

Shave The Beard. 53

FEW ADVICE FOR HUSBAND AND WIFE.........56

BEG FOR PARDON

بِسْمِ اللهِ الرَّحْمنِ الرَّحِيمِ

If My Allah Asks Me 'Have You (Any) Shyness In Disobeying Me?'

You Conceal Your Sins From My Creation And With Sins You Come To Me.

So How Will I Answer? O Woe To Me And Who Shall Protect Me?

I Keep Averting My Soul With Thoughts Of Hope From Time To Time.

And I Forget What Is To Come After Death And What Is To Come After I Am Shrouded.

As If I Am Gaurenteed Life (Eternally) And The Death Will Not Come To Me.

And When The Severe Stupor Of Death Overtakes Me, Who Will Protect Me?

I Looked At The Faces, Is There Not From Amongst Them Who Will Ransom Me?

I Will Be Asked Regarding What I Have Prepared In My Life To Save Me (On The Day Of Judgment)

Then How Will I Answer After I Have Neglected My Religion.

Woe To Me! Did I Not Hear The Speech Of Allah Inviting Me?

Did I Not Hear What Came In (The Chapters Of) 'Qaaf' And Yaa'seen' ?

Did I Not Hear About The Day Of Gathering, The Day Of Assemble And The Day Of Judgement?

Did I Not Hear The Crier Of Death Inviting Me, Calling Me?

So 'O My Lord, A Slave (Turning To You) I Have Repented, So Who Then Shall Shelter Me?

Except A Lord Extensive In Forgiveness To The Truth He Will Guide Me.

I Have Come To You (In Repentance) So Have Mercy On Me, And Make Heavy My Scales (With Good Deeds)

And Lighten My Account, You Are The Best Of Who Will Bring Me To Account.

ABOUT THE BOOK

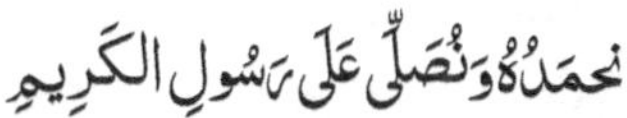

Etiquette of Intimacy in Islam delves into the sacred teachings of Islam concerning intimate relationships, providing profound insights and guidance on navigating this fundamental aspect of human existence. Within the framework of Islamic principles, this book addresses various facets of intimacy, offering clarity, wisdom, and practical advice for individuals seeking to uphold the highest moral standards in their personal lives.

From fostering kindness and compassion towards one's spouse to the significance of performing Salah together as a couple, each chapter explores essential etiquettes that contribute to the harmony and spiritual elevation of marital relationships. Readers will discover the significance of dua during intimate moments, learn the proper manner of engaging in marital relations, and understand the boundaries and prohibitions outlined in Islam regarding intimate conduct.

Etiquette of Intimacy in Islam courageously tackles sensitive topics such as the prohibition of anal intercourse, the permissibility of joint showers with one's spouse, and the prohibition of marital relations during menstruation. Through a careful examination of Quranic teachings and authentic Hadiths, this book provides clarity on often misunderstood aspects of intimate conduct, empowering readers to make informed choices that align with Islamic values.

Whether you are a newlywed couple seeking guidance, a seasoned spouse looking to deepen your understanding of Islamic principles, or an individual striving to lead a righteous life, **Etiquette of Intimacy in Islam** serves as a beacon of knowledge and inspiration. It offers a roadmap for cultivating intimacy rooted in love, respect, and devotion, in accordance with the timeless teachings of Islam.

Embark on a transformative journey towards a fulfilling and spiritually enriching intimate relationship guided by the profound wisdom encapsulated within the pages of **Etiquette of Intimacy in Islam.**

PREFACE

Welcome to ***Etiquette of Intimacy in Islam***, a comprehensive exploration of the sacred principles guiding intimate relationships within the framework of Islam. In a world where the understanding of intimacy is often overshadowed by societal norms and cultural influences, this book endeavors to shed light on the profound teachings of Islam regarding this deeply personal aspect of human experience.

Intimacy is a divine gift bestowed upon humanity, designed to foster love, connection, and spiritual growth. However, navigating the intricacies of intimate relationships requires knowledge, wisdom, and a steadfast adherence to Islamic values.

In this book, we embark on a journey through the teachings of Islam concerning intimacy, exploring the etiquette, principles, and responsibilities incumbent upon individuals within marital relationships. From the significance of purity and modesty to the etiquettes of marital intimacy and the sacred bond of marriage, each chapter delves into essential aspects of intimate conduct as outlined in the Quran and Sunnah.

It is my sincere hope that *Etiquette of Intimacy in Islam* serves as a guiding light for individuals seeking to cultivate healthy, fulfilling, and spiritually enriching intimate relationships. May this book inspire reflection, foster understanding, and empower readers to approach intimacy with reverence, mindfulness, and adherence to the timeless wisdom of Islam.

With humility and gratitude,

بِسْمِ اللهِ الرَّحْمٰنِ الرَّحِيمِ

نَحْمَدُهُ وَنُصَلِّى عَلَى رَسُولِ الْكَرِيمِ

All praise is due to Allah Almighty who said in His Holy Book:

وَمِنْ آيَاتِهِ أَنْ خَلَقَ لَكُمْ مِّنْ أَنْفُسِكُمْ أَزْوَاجًا لِّتَسْكُنُوا إِلَيْهَا وَجَعَلَ بَيْنَكُمْ مُّوَدَّةً وَرَحْمَةً [٠/ الروم]

> "And among His signs is that He created your wives from among yourselves so that you may find peace with Him, and He placed love and affection between you."

And blessings and peace be upon Muhammad, who said.

Marry a woman who loves more and gives birth to more children. I will boast against (other) prophets because of your abundance.

After that, when the married man intends to have intercourse with his wife, Islam has mentioned some manners for him. Most people ignore them or don't know about them.

It pleased me that on the occasion of my brother's marriage, I should mention these manners in the form of an excellent booklet, so that in light of this, my brother and other Muslims should follow this Shariah of Muhammad (peace be upon). May God bless him and grant him peace. It is easy to be what the Lord of the Universe has revealed to them. At the end of this book, I have also drawn attention to some of the issues that many people who are getting married today seem to be committing.

I pray to Allah (subhanahu wa ta'ala) to make it profitable and purify this effort for Himself; surely He is the Giver of good and the Most Merciful.

It should be noted that there are many manners of intimacy, but in this haste, we consider it appropriate to mention only those manners that are proven by the blessed Sunnah of Muhammad, the Messenger of Allah, peace be upon him. There is not even the slightest doubt about their denial in terms of authenticity. My effort is only so that (the one getting married) can follow these teachings with full insight and full conviction. I pray to Allah Ta'ala to inaugurate his married life with the followers of the Sunnah, to make his (our brother's) life happy, and to include him among His servants, whose attributes Allah Ta'ala has set in His will. It has been stated in His Holy Book.

$$رَبَّنَا هَبْ لَنَا مِنْ أَزْوَاجِنَا وَذُرِّيَّاتِنَا قُرَّةَ أَعْيُنٍ وَاجْعَلْنَا لِلْمُتَّقِينَ إِمَامًا (٥)$$

$$الفرقان: ٧٤$$

And those who say, "Our Lord, grant us from among our wives and offspring comfort to our eyes and make us an example for the righteous."

It is certain that the good end is only for the righteous. Allah Almighty said:

$$إِنَّ الْمُتَّقِينَ فِي ظِلَالٍ وَعُيُونٍ ﴾$$

$$وَفَوَاكِهَ مِمَّا يَشْتَهُونَ ﴾$$

$$كُلُوا وَاشْرَبُوا هَنِيئًا بِمَا كُنْتُمْ تَعْمَلُونَ ﴾$$

$$إِنَّا كَذَلِكَ نَجْزِي الْمُحْسِنِينَ ﴾$$

"Of course, the God-fearing will be amid shades and streams,

and fruits of their desire.

It will be said to them, "Eat and drink with pleasure because of what you used to do."

This is how We reward those who do good deeds."

See etiquette of Intimacy in Islam in the next lines.

KINDNESS TO WIFE

It is recommended for a man, when he goes to his wife, to treat her with kindness, for example, by offering her something to eat or drink.

Asma bint Yazid Sakin says:

I decorated Sayyida Aisha for the Messenger of Allah, may God bless him and grant him peace, and sent a message that she should come and meet him. The Messenger of Allah, may Allah bless him and grant him peace, came and sat next to Aisha, and a large bowl of milk was presented to her. The Messenger of Allah first drank from it himself and then brought it to Aisha, but her head bowed in shame. I scolded them and said, Take the cup from the Holy Prophet's hand, on which she took the cup and drank some milk. Then the Prophet (peace and blessings of Allah be upon him) said to Hazrat Aisha (may Allah be pleased with her) to give this to her sister. Asmaa (may Allah be pleased with her) says: I said, O Messenger of Allah, may Allah bless him and grant him peace; take it and drink it yourself first, then give it to me. He took the cup, drank some milk from it, and returned the rest to me. She says: I sat down and began to spin the cup so that I could place my lips on the place where the Messenger of Allah, may God bless him and grant him peace, drank from his blessed lips. Then he (peace and blessings of Allah be upon him) said to the other women who were with me, "You also drink." They started saying: We don't need it. He said, "Do not mix lies and hunger."

PRAYING FOR THE WIFE

Placing hands on the head of the wife and praying for her.

Before sleeping with his wife, the groom should place his hand on the front of her head, recite the name of Allah, say (Bismillah), pray for blessings, and read the following dua of the Holy Prophet (peace and blessings of Allah be upon him).

The Prophet (peace be upon him) said:

When one of you marries a woman or buys a slave, hold her by the forehead, mention the name of Allah, and pray for blessings.

Read this dua:

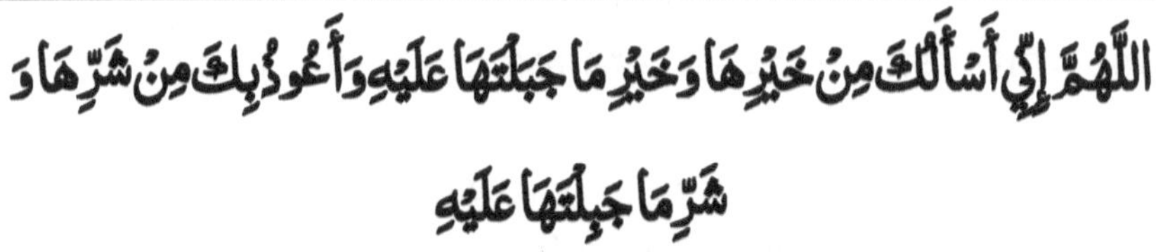

O Allah, I ask You for his good and the good for which You created him, and I seek Your refuge from his evil and from the evil for which You created him.

PERFORM SALAT WITH WIFE

It is mustahabb for both husband and wife to pray two rak'ahs together because it was narrated from the Salaf as-Saliheen. There are two pieces of evidence in this.

First.

Abi Saeed, who is a slave of Abi Asyad, says:I married in a state of slavery. I invited the Companions of the

Prophet (peace be upon him)., including Ibn Masood Abu Dharr and Huzaifa; may Allah be pleased with them. When Abu Dharr went forward to lead the congregation, the Companions told him to stay. They said, Should I really stay?The Companions said, Yes. (Abi Saeed) said, They put me ahead even though I was a slave. He told me and said, When your wife comes to you, perform two rak'ahs with her, then ask Allah for the well-being of her. And asking to be safe from his evil. After that, the matter is up to both of you.

Second .

It is narrated from Hazrat Shaqiq that a man named Abu Hurayz came to him and said, I have married a young virgin girl, and I am afraid that she will hate me. Abdullah bin Masoud (may Allah be pleased with him) said: Verily, love is from Allah, and unbelief is from Satan. Because He wants to make those things undesirable for you, which Allah has made lawful for you. When he comes to you, order him to pray two rak'ahs behind you.

Another hadith is:

That this story is narrated from Ibn Masud, may Allah bless him and grant him peace, that he said to him, then say it like this:

اللَّهُمَّ بَارِكْ لِي فِي أَهْلِي، وَبَارِكْ لَهُمْ فِيَّ اللَّهُمَّ أَجْمَعْ بَيْنَنَا مَا جَمَعْتَ بِخَيْرٍ وَفَرِّقْ بَيْنَنَا إِذَا فَرَّقْتَ إِلَى خَيْرٍ

O Allah! Bless me in my family and bless them in me. O Allah! Bring us both together for good, and when you separate us, do it only for good.

DUA OF INTIMATE

When he intends to have intercourse with his wife. So recite this dua:

بِسُمِ اللَّهِ اللَّهُمَّ جَنِّبْنَا الشَّيْطَانَ وَجَنِّبِ الشَّيْطَانَ مَا رَزَقْتَنَا

With the name of Allah. O Allah! Protect us from Satan, and whoever gives us sustenance (children) also protects us from Satan.

The Prophet (peace be upon him) said:

If during this time (Allah) grants them both children, Satan can never harm him.

HOW TO HAVE INTERCOURSE?

It is permissible for him to have intercourse with his wife in (place of birth) whether it is from any direction (from the front or from behind).

The proof of this claim is this statement of Allah Almighty:

نِسَاؤُكُمْ حَرْثٌ لَّكُمْ فَأْتُوا حَرْثَكُمْ أَنَّى شِئْتُمْ

"Your women are your fields, come to your fields as you wish."

That is, as you wish, from the front or from behind (in the front part) have intercourse.

There are many hadiths related to it. It is sufficient to mention only two here.

First.

narrated by Hazrat Jabir (may Allah be pleased with him):
The Jews used to say that if a man has intercourse with his wife behind her back (in the front part), the child will be born a squint.

This verse was revealed to him:

نِسَاؤُكُمْ حَرْثٌ لَّكُمْ فَأْتُوا حَرْثَكُمْ أَنَّى شِئْتُمْ

"Your women are your fields, come to your fields as you wish."

On this, Muhammad (peace and blessings of Allah be upon him) said: From the front or from the back, except that in (the place of birth).

Second.

It is narrated from Hazrat Ibn Abbas (may Allah be pleased with him).

In Madinah, there was a tribe of Ansari who worshiped idols. People of the Book (Jews) also lived with them. The Jews considered themselves superior to the People of the Book Ansari tribe on the basis of knowledge. The people of the Ansari tribe followed him in many things. People of the Book used to establish a relationship with a woman (by lying down). It was a cause of great sorrow for the woman. In this matter, too, the Ansar followed the Jews. Qureshi people use various methods to relate to their women and enjoy sexual intercourse. They used to establish relationships with women by going from front to back and lying down. When the emigrant Companions came to Medina, one of them married a woman of the Ansar. He (according to his custom) wanted to have intercourse with her, but she refused. And she said, With us, only one method of relationship is established. Do the same, or stay away from me. The woman kept insisting on the same, and the matter escalated. When this matter reached the Prophet, may Allah bless him and grant him peace, Allah revealed this verse.

نِسَاؤُكُمْ حَرْثٌ لَّكُمْ فَأْتُوا حَرْثَكُمْ أَنَّى شِئْتُمْ

> "Your women are your fields, come to your fields as you wish."
>
> That is, take advantage of going back and forth or lying down, but with the condition that sexual intercourse takes place at the place of birth.

FORBIDDEN IN THE ANUS

It is forbidden for a husband to have sexual intercourse in his wife's anus (place of excrement).

The reason for this is the meaning of the previous verse

نِسَاؤُكُمْ حَرْثٌ لَّكُمْ فَأْتُوا حَرْثَكُمْ أَنَّى شِئْتُمْ

Similarly, the mentioned hadiths and many other hadiths indicate this.

First Hadith:

Hazrat Umm Salma narrates:

When the emigrants came to Medina, they arranged marriages with their women. The emigrants had sexual intercourse with women lying upside down on the ground (or placing their hands on the ground or knees). A man from among the emigrants intended to have intercourse with an Ansari woman in this way, so she refused and said, "I cannot do this before I ask the Messenger of Allah; may God bless him and grant him peace." She attended the Prophet's service but was shy about asking questions. Then Umm Salma asked the Prophet (peace and blessings of Allah be upon him) and this verse was revealed

نِسَاؤُكُمْ حَرْثٌ لَّكُمْ فَأْتُوا حَرْثَكُمْ أَنَّى شِئْتُمْ

And the Prophet (peace and blessings of Allah be upon him) said, No, but in the same place (place of birth).

Second Hadith:

It is narrated from Hazrat Ibn Abbas (may Allah be pleased with him).

Hazrat Umar bin Al-Khattab (RA) came to the Prophet (PBUH) and said, "O Messenger of Allah (PBUH), I have been killed." The Prophet (PBUH) asked, "What killed you?" He began to say, "Tonight I turned my head upside down. The Prophet (peace and blessings of Allah be upon him) remained silent and did not answer, so this verse was revealed to the Messenger of Allah (peace and blessings of Allah be upon him)."

نِسَاؤُكُمۡ حَرۡثٌ لَّكُمۡ فَأۡتُوا حَرۡثَكُمۡ أَنَّىٰ شِئۡتُمۡ

Muhammad (PBUH) said:

Come from the front or come from the back, but avoid anus. And avoid menstruating women.

Third Hadith:

It is narrated from Hazrat Khuzima bin Thabit (RA).

A man asked women about intercourse in the anus. Or if a man has sexual intercourse with his woman in the anus, how is it? The Prophet (peace and blessings of Allah be upon him) said: It is permissible. When that man turned to leave, the Prophet (peace and blessings of Allah be upon him) called him or ordered him to be called. What did you said? About which place did you ask? You asked about the woman's place of birth, or anus? What do you mean from behind in the woman's front (place of birth)? This is permissible, and if it is in the woman's anus (ass)? So it is illegal. Verily, Allah is not ashamed of the truth, so do not have intercourse with women in the anus.

The fourth hadith:

Allah Ta'ala will not even look at a man who has sex in his wife's anus.

The fifth hadith:

Cursed is the man who has intercourse in the anus of women.

Sixth Hadith:

A man who has sexual intercourse with a menstruating woman or anus of a woman or confirmed the words of a soothsayer (astrologer). So he denied the goodness (the Qur'an) revealed to Muhammad (peace and blessings of Allah be upon him).

WHEN INTERCOURSE AGAIN, PERFORM ABLUTION

When a man has sexual intercourse with his wife in a lawful manner and intends to have sexual intercourse again, he should perform ablution in view of the following decree of the Prophet (peace and blessings of Allah be upon him). When one of you has intercourse with his wife, Then, if he wants to have sexual intercourse again, he should perform ablution. There is a tradition that he should perform ablution between two times. There is a tradition that performing ablution as a prayer is a cause of greater readiness for sexual intercourse again.

TAKING A JOINT SHOWER WITH THE SPOUSE

It is permissible for a husband and wife to perform ghusl together in the same place, even if they are looking at each other. The following hadiths can be presented as evidence in this issue.

First:

Hazrat Aisha (may Allah be pleased with her) says: I and the Messenger of Allah (peace and blessings of Allah be upon him) used to bathe together in the same vessel. Our hands were touching each other inside the vessel. If you were quick, I would have asked. Leave it for me too. Leave it for me too. And she says, "Both of us were in the state of janabat (in the state of obligatory shower (gusal)).

Second:

There is a hadith on the authority of Muawiya bin Hayda (RA).

I said, O Messenger of Allah, may God bless him and grant him peace. With whom we hide our veils (private parts) and with whom we open. The Prophet (peace and blessings of Allah be upon him) said: "Protect your private parts apart from your wife and your maidservant. They say, I said, If some people are with some e people, (Men be with men.) Then the Prophet (peace and blessings of Allah be upon him) said: If you have the power that no one should see your private parts, then no one should see them. They say, I said, sometimes a person is alone. The Messenger of Allah, may Allah bless him and grant him peace, said: Allah has more right that people should be ashamed of Him.

INTERCOURSE WITH A MENSTRUATING WOMAN IS PROHIBITED.

Intercourse with a woman during menstruation is forbidden because Allah says:

وَيَسْأَلُونَكَ عَنِ الْمَحِيضِ قُلْ هُوَ أَذًى فَاعْتَزِلُوا النِّسَاءَ فِي الْمَحِيضِ وَلَا تَقْرَبُوهُنَّ حَتَّى يَطْهُرْنَ فَإِذَا تَطَهَّرْنَ فَأْتُوهُنَّ مِنْ حَيْثُ أَمَرَكُمُ اللَّهُ إِنَّ اللَّهَ يُحِبُّ التَّوَّابِينَ وَيُحِبُّ الْمُتَطَهِّرِينَ

They ask you about menstruation. Say: "It is an impurity. So, keep away from women during menstruation; and do not have intimacy with them until they are cleansed. But when they are cleansed, then go to them from where Allah has commanded you. Surely Allah loves those who are most repenting, and loves those who keep themselves pure.

Many hadiths are proven in this issue.

First

Muhammad (PBUH) said:

A man who has sexual intercourse with a menstruating woman or anus of a woman or confirmed the words of a soothsayer (astrologer). So he denied the goodness (the Qur'an) revealed to Muhammad (peace and blessings of Allah be upon him).

Second

It is narrated from Hazrat Anas bin Malik, may Allah be pleased with him, that he said: If a woman's menstruation began among the Jews, they would throw her out of the house and neither eat nor drink with her. And they didn't even let him come inside the house. When the Prophet (peace and blessings of Allah be upon him) was asked about this, Allah revealed this order in the Holy Qur'an.

> وَيَسْأَلُونَكَ عَنِ الْمَحِيضِ قُلْ هُوَ أَذًى فَاعْتَزِلُوا النِّسَاءَ فِي الْمَحِيضِ ..... (الخ)

The Prophet (peace and blessings of Allah be upon him) said, "Keep them with you in your homes. And take advantage of them in every way except sexual intercourse."

The Jews said: This man (Muhammad, may God bless him and grant him peace) does not want to leave any work in which he does not oppose us. Sawasid bin Hudair and Ibad bin Bashir came to the service of the

Holy Prophet (peace and blessings of Allah be upon him) and began to say: The Jews are saying such and such things. Shouldn't we marry (sexual intercourse) women during the days of menstruation? The blessed face of the Prophet (peace and blessings of Allah be upon him) changed so much that we felt that the Prophet (peace and blessings of Allah be upon him) was angry with both of them. They both left. (They had just gone some distance) that a bowl of milk sent by the Prophet (peace and blessings of Allah be upon him) came in front of them. which was a gift for them, the Prophet (peace and blessings of Allah be upon him) sent milk after them and fed them. We are sure that you are not angry with them.

ATONEMENT FOR THE ONE WHO HAS SEXUAL INTERCOURSE WHILE MENSTRUATING

Intercourse during the period of menstruation is forbidden and unlawful. If this sin has been expunged with the consent of the spouses, then both of them have become sinners; both of them should seek forgiveness, and it is better that they give some charity after that. So good deeds wash away sins. If you can afford it, donate one dinar (4.374 grams of gold coin) or half a dinar (or its value).

Ibn Abbas (may Allah be pleased with him) narrates.

That the Messenger of Allah (peace and blessings of Allah be upon him) said: Whoever has intercourse with a menstruating woman should give one or half a dinar in charity.

HOW MUCH BENEFIT CAN BE TAKEN FROM A MENSTRUATING WOMAN?

It is permissible for him (the husband) to take advantage of all of the body of a menstruating woman except her private parts.

There are many hadiths related to this issue.

First
The Prophet (peace and blessings of Allah be upon him) said: Do everything except sexual intercourse.

Secondly

Hazrat Aisha (may Allah be pleased with her) says: The Messenger of Allah, may God bless him and grant him peace, used to order us women during the days of menstruation to fasten their azar band tightly, and then her husband should lie with her, and sometimes they would say that he should do (everything except sexual intercourse).

Third

There is a tradition from some wives of the Prophet, peace and blessings be upon him, that they say: Indeed, when the Prophet (peace and blessings of Allah be upon him) intended to take advantage of her menstruation (wife), he would put a cloth over her private parts and then do whatever he intended.

HOW LONG AFTER A WOMAN IS PURIFIED IS IT ACCEPTABLE TO HAVE SEX WITH HER?

When a woman is free from menstruation and her bleeding stops, So sexual intercourse with him is permissible, provided he performs ghusl, washes the spot of blood thoroughly, or performs ablution. If she arranges any of these things, she will become pure. At that time, intercourse with him will be permissible. The reason for this is the statement of Allah Subhanahu wa Ta'ala, which has been mentioned in the previous verse.

> فَإِذَا تَطَهَّرْنَ فَأْتُوهُنَّ مِنْ حَيْثُ أَمَرَكُمُ اللَّهُ إِنَّ اللَّهَ يُحِبُّ التَّوَّابِينَ وَيُحِبُّ الْمُتَطَهِّرِينَ

> When they are cleansed, then go to them from where Allah has commanded you. Surely Allah loves those who are most repenting, and loves those who keep themselves pure.

AZAL LEGAL OR ILLEGAL?

Azal means to expel the sperm out of the wife's private parts (place of birth).

One of the main purposes of marriage in Shariat-i-Mutahrah is procreation, and an abundance of children is desirable. This is the reason why, in the blessed hadith, it is encouraged to marry a woman who gives birth to more children. Therefore, Azal without an excuse is undesirable; however, if there is an excuse, Azal with the permission of the wife will be permissible without exception, and in some situations, it is possible even without the permission of the wife.

A few reasons are listed below in the presence of which "Azal" block relief is permissible:

1:

If a woman is so weak that she is unable to bear the burden of pregnancy, is unable to endure the pains of pregnancy and childbirth, or is afraid of severe weakness and weakness after the birth of the child, then "Azal" is permissible.

2:

For a proper interval between two children so that the child can receive proper care from the mother and so that the mother's milk does not become dangerous and harmful to the first child due to the pregnancy of the second child.

3:

If the woman is immoral and hard-tempered and the husband intends to divorce her and fears that her immorality will increase after the birth of a child, in such a case, Azal is permissible.

4:

In the same way, if there is a fear of loss of life or faith of the child due to being on a long journey or being in Darul-Harb, then "Azal" is permissible.

In the above-mentioned cases, it is correct to adopt such a method of Azal that can prevent pregnancy temporarily. So that the cycle of rebirth and reproduction can be continued whenever desired. Removal of the uterus by operations, sterilization, or adopting any method that completely destroys the ability to produce children is not permissible in the Shariah.

WHAT IS THE INTENTION OF A HUSBAND AND WIFE IN MARRIAGE?

Both of them should intend to avoid sin through marriage and stay away from things forbidden by Allah subhanahu wa ta'ala so that the relationship between husband and wife also becomes charity for them.

The proof of this is the hadith of Abu Dharr (may God be pleased with him).

Some of the companions of the Holy Prophet (Sallallahu Alaihi Wasallam) said: O Messenger of Allah (Sallallahu Alaihi Wasallam), the people of wealth (rich and wealthy) have taken a lot of reward. They pray and fast like us. And (as well as) they give charity from their wealth. The Prophet (peace and blessings of Allah be upon him) said: "Hasn't Allah made (certain things) a charity for you? Indeed, every glorification is a charity. Every Takbeer is a charity. Saying there is no god but Allah is a charity. Commanding good deeds is a charity." Preventing evil is a charity. Your (intimacy with your wife) is a charity. The Companions said, O Messenger of Allah, when one of us fulfills his lust, is this also a charity for him? The Prophet (peace and blessings of Allah be upon him) said, What do you think if he establishes this relationship in a forbidden place, then there is no sin on him? The companions asked: Why not? The Prophet (peace be upon him) said: "Therefore, when If he establishes this relationship with a lawful place (wife or concubine), it is a reward for him. Apart from this, the Prophet (peace and blessings of Allah be upon him) enumerated many things and called them Sadaqah. And at the end, he said, "Chasht. Two rakats are sufficient for all of them.

SPOUSES SHOULD NOT SHARE THEIR SECRETS WITH OTHERS.

It is forbidden for both of them to tell the secrets of their relationship to others. There are two hadiths in this regard.

First:

Muhammad (PBUH) said:
On the Day of Resurrection, the worst person in the sight of Allah Ta'ala is the one who comes to his wife and she comes to him, then they tell people about their secret relationship.

Second:

Hum Asmaa bint Yazid was sitting next to the Messenger of Allah (peace and blessings of Allah be upon him), while other men and women were also present.
The Prophet (PBUH) said:

Perhaps some describe what they do to their wives. And maybe some women describe what they do to their husbands? People were silent after hearing this. I said, O Messenger of Allah, may God bless him and grant him peace. That's exactly how it is. Men do the same, and women do the same. The Holy Prophet (peace and blessings of Allah be upon him) said, "Do not do this at all. It is like a male devil meets a female devil on the road and covers her there (committing adultery). While people are looking at them.

SHARIAH PROCEDURE OF MARRIAGE

The best way to get married is to get married in a mosque. Then, after the marriage, the girl should be brought to the groom's house through her mehram relatives (Relatives from whom veiling is not necessary, i.e., parents, siblings, etc.). A traditional barat (in which a large number of people go from the boy's house) is not a sunnah procedure of marriage.

The Prophet (peace and blessings of Allah be upon him) sent a man (Sharhbeel bin Hasna) to bring the bride to the wedding of Hazrat Umm Habiba bint Abi Sufyan (RA), but he did not go to the bride's house.

In the same way, it was customary for the Messenger of Allah (peace and blessings of Allah be upon him) and his Companions (may Allah be pleased with them) to marry that the girl's father or guardian would prepare the girl and bring her to the house of the groom himself or another trusted relative. As it is mentioned in the Hadith of Bukhari Sharif about the marriage of Hazrat Aisha, her mother brought her to the house of the Holy Prophet. He (PBUH) did not visit himself, nor did he send anyone. Similarly, Hazrat Fatima (RA) was sent by the Prophet (SAW) along with Hazrat Umm Ayman (RA), (who was the freed slave of the Prophet (SAW)). Therefore, one should avoid common marriage, but there is no harm in avoiding illicit affairs with close relatives and certain friends.

DRUMMING, SINGING, FIREWORKS, AND MIXED GATHERINGS ON THE OCCASION OF MARRIAGE.

Playing Drums, Playing Songs Is Forbidden In Shariat.

In the Holy Quran:

وَمِنَ النَّاسِ مَنْ يَّشْتَرِي لَهْوَ الْحَدِيثِ لِيُضِلَّ عَنْ سَبِيلِ اللَّهِ بِغَيْرِ عِلْمٍ

وَيَتَّخِذَهَا هُزُوًا أُولَئِكَ لَهُمْ عَذَابٌ مُّهِينٌ (سورة لقمان:

There is a man among the people who buys discourses of distracting amusements, so that he may mislead (people) from the Way of Allah, and make a mockery of it. For such people there is a disgraceful punishment.

If Hazrat Abdullah bin Masoud (RA) was asked about this verse, he used to swear that "لهو الحديث" means singing.

It was narrated from Hazrat Jabir that the Messenger of Allah, may God bless him and grant him peace, said: Singing creates hypocrisy in the heart like water makes crops grow.

It was narrated from Hazrat Nafi that I was going to a place with Hazrat Abdullah bin Umar, and when he heard the sound of a flute, he put his fingers in his ears and started walking on one side of the road. He said, O Nafi, are you listening to something? I said, No, he took his fingers out of his ear and said, "I was going with the Messenger of Allah; may Allah bless him and grant him peace. The Prophet heard the sound of the flute and did the same as I did."

These arguments made it clear that playing drums and playing music is haram.

Fireworks, Air Firing.

Marriage is a pure and respectable relationship between husband and wife which has been ordered to be publicized in a legitimate way by the Messenger of Allah ﷺ, for example, marriage in Jamia Masjid. However, it is forbidden to advertise in a way that contains Shariah corruptions and myths. Fireworks, air-firing on the occasions of marriage, etc. involve many evils, such as loss of property, harassment, spreading fear, as well as causing loss of life or property, violation of the law, etc. Therefore, fireworks, air firing are not allowed to express happiness.

Tahafat al-Ahuzi is in the hadeeth of Sunan Tirmidhi:

$$\text{قَالَ رَسُولُ اللَّهِ صَلَّى اللَّهُ عَلَيْهِ وَسَلَّمَ: «أَعْلِنُوا هَذَا النِّكَاحَ، وَاجْعَلُوهُ فِي الْمَسَاجِدِ، وَاضْرِبُوا عَلَيْهِ بِالدُّفُوفِ»}$$

Therefore, it is known that air-firing and fireworks are not permissible.

Mixed Gathering.

Not taking care of the Shariah veil on the occasion of marriage, etc., holding a mixed gathering—these are illegal acts, and the ceremonies in which illegitimacy and sins are committed are against the Shariah.

Allah Almighty says in the Holy Quran:

يَآ أَيُّهَا النَّبِيُّ قُلْ لِّأَزْوَاجِكَ وَبَنٰتِكَ وَنِسَآءِ الْمُؤْمِنِيْنَ يُدْنِيْنَ عَلَيْهِنَّ مِنْ جَلَابِيْبِهِنَّ ذٰلِكَ أَدْنٰى أَنْ يُّعْرَفْنَ فَلَا يُؤْذَيْنَ وَكَانَ اللّٰهُ غَفُوْرًا رَّحِيْمًا". (سورۃ الاحزاب، آیت نمبر: 59)

O prophet, tell your wives and your daughters and the women of the believers that they should draw down their shawls over them. That will make it more likely that they are recognized, hence not teased. And Allah is MostForgiving, Very-Merciful.

The aforesaid verse is very important in the commands of "veil", it clearly commands "face veil".

The commentators have clarified this issue in great detail in their interpretation of this verse, so from the time of the revelation of the said verse until now, the Companions, may Allah bless them and grant them peace. And the jurists of all Masaliks have been explaining the same meaning of this blessed verse. Therefore, when going out of the house, it is necessary for a woman to cover her whole body, including her face, in front of a non-mahram with a large veil or a thick burqa; only her eyes are allowed to be open to see the way.

Therefore, it was found that when a veil is ordered in normal circumstances, it is illegal to hold a mixed gathering on the occasion of marriage.

NONE MUSLIM MARRIAGE RITUALS

1. Mayoo.
2. Henna.
3. On the day of marriage, a necklace (only the father-in-law will wear it) and money have to be given.
4. fed milk.
5. Kajal applied (sister-in-law will apply) and money has to be paid.
6. The gate was closed.
7. Shoe hide. Etc.

All the above-mentioned rituals can be abandoned and reformed. These are the rituals of NONE MUSLIM that have been embedded in us Muslims, and it is necessary to abandon them.

The Prophet (peace be upon him) said:

> عن ابن عمر رضي الله عنهما قال: قال رسول الله صلى الله عليه وسلم: من تشبه بقوم فهو منهم
>
> Whoever takes on the likeness of a nation is one of them.

Therefore, from this hadith, it is known that all the rituals of the Gentiles should be abandoned.

PLACING THE QUR'AN ON THE BRIDE'S HEAD AT THE TIME OF MARRIAGE

Keeping the Quran on the bride's head at the time of marriage has no place in Islamic law, and this ritual should be avoided.

WALIMA SUNNAH OR WAJIB?

"Walima" is a mustahab act, not a wajib act.

When Is Walima Sunnah After Three Days Or After One Day?

Walima:

This food is said to be eaten after the gathering of the husband and wife, i.e., after the wedding night, until the third day of the wedding night. If the arrangements can be made on the first day after the wedding night, then the first day is the best. After the third day, the Walima will be counted only as a feast.

If there are many guests, or instead of inviting the guests by holding a walima once, guests come and go one after the other, then the walima food can be fed continuously   for   three   days. Holy Prophet ﷺ In the same way, he did Walima for three days in his marriage with Hazrat Safiyyah. Purpose: Walimah should be done in one day, or, according to the alias, up to three consecutive days; both   are   valid. But in feeding food for three consecutive days, the condition should be observed that there should be no show-off or extravagance in it; rather, this matter should be done with the intention of following the Sunnah as much as possible. There is a hadith: "On the first day Walimah is right, on the second day it is good, and on the (consecutive) third day it is hearing and showing off."

Walima Is Permissible Even Without Meat.

Walima can be done only with what is available to man, even if it does not contain meat.

Hadith Of Hazrat Anas (May Allah Be Pleased With Him):

The Prophet (PBUH) stayed three nights between Khaibar and Madinah. During this time, he married Hazrat Safiya (RA). He invited the Muslims for Walima, although there was neither meat nor bread in it. The Prophet (peace and blessings of Allah be upon him) ordered to lay a leather table, and the table was laid. (There is a tradition that the land was cleaned to be thoroughly cleaned.) Then a leather table was brought and placed on the cleaned ground. Then dates, dried milk, and butter were placed on it, which the people ate to their satisfaction.

Forbidden To Invite Only Rich People To Walima.

Ignoring the poor and inviting only the wealthy to the feast of Walimah is prohibited due to the following Hadith of the Prophet:

The worst of all meals is a feast of Walimah in which the rich are brought in and the poor are neglected.And whoever does not accept the invitation has disobeyed Allah and His Messenger (peace and blessings of Allah be upon him).

AVOID AFFAIRS AGAINST SHARIAT

A human should avoid opposing Sharia on this (joyful) occasion, especially when many people in the present age have made it a habit to oppose Sharia on such occasions.

Even because of the silence of the scholars, many people think that such matters are permissible. Below, we are warning about some actions that are against Shariah. See

Plucking Of Eyebrow Hair Etc.

Some women try to make their eyebrows look like an arc or crescent (moon) by plucking the hair of their eyebrows to enhance their beauty. The Prophet (peace and blessings of Allah be upon him) forbade this act and cursed the woman who did it. The Prophet (peace and blessings of Allah be upon him) said: Allah has cursed those who knead (the body) and those who knead (the body), those who braid hair, those who pull out facial hair, those who pluck them, and those who spread their teeth for beauty—those who change the creation of Allah.

Longer Nails And Nail Polish.

Another ugly and bad habit that has been ingrained in our Muslim women by the immoral women of Europe is to polish the nails and make them long. It is the polished red color, etc., that is called (manicure) today. Some young Muslims also seem to be suffering from this disease. Where this act is equivalent to changing the natural creation of Allah Ta'ala, then the perpetrator deserves the curse of Allah. Moreover, it has similarities with non-Muslim women. There are many hadiths on the prohibition of this act. One of them is that Whosoever likened himself to a nation, he would be one of them. This habit is also against nature.

> "فِطْرَةَ اللهِ الَّتِي فَطَرَ النَّاسَ عَلَيْهَا" (سورة الروم)
>
> The nature of Allah on which He created people.

The Prophet (peace and blessings of Allah be upon him) said:

"Five things are of nature: circumcision, cleaning the pubic hair, trimming the moustache, trimming the nails, and plucking the hair of the armpits."

There is a tradition that cleaning the pubic hair, trimming the moustache, trimming the nails, and plucking the armpit hair.

And Hazrat Anas says:

The Prophet (peace and blessings of Allah be upon him) set a time for us to trim our moustaches, trim our nails, pluck the hair from our armpits, and clean our pubic hair, so that we should not miss them for more than forty days.

Shave The Beard.

Similarly, another abominable act is shaving the beard. Most Muslim men shave their beards in imitation of the infidels of Europe. This act is at least as ugly as growing the nails of women. Now the matter has reached this point where people feel shame and disrespect. The groom goes to the bride, and he has not shaved his beard.

Shaving the beard is against Islam for several reasons.

1

Changing the creation of Allah Almighty:

Allah Almighty said about Satan:Allah has cursed him. He said, "I will mislead a certain number of your servants." I will continue to lead them astray. I will give them false desires, and I will teach them to tear off the ears of animals, and I will tell them to distort the creation created by Allah, so whoever abandons Allah and makes Satan his friend, he will be in clear loss."

This is a clear argument that changing the creation of Allah without His permission is, in reality, obedience to Satan and disobedience to Allah. There is absolutely no doubt that those who shave their beards to look beautiful deserve the curse of the Messenger of Allah (peace and blessings of Allah be upon him) in the same way that women deserve the curse for changing their creations for the sake of beauty. Both are guilty of the same sin." I have used the word Allah's permission because someone could have the illusion that removing pubic hair, etc. is also included in this interpretation, but in reality it is not. It is permitted. Rather, it has been declared obligatory.

2

Shaving the beard is a clear violation of the Prophet's command.

Muhammad (PBUH) said:

Trim the mustache well and grow the beard.

3

There is an analogy with the disbelievers.

The Prophet (peace and blessings of Allah be upon him) saidTrim the mustache, hang the beard, and oppose the Magi.

4

Similarities with women:Indeed, the Prophet (peace be upon him) has cursed those men who resemble women and those women who resemble men. There is no doubt that to shave off the beard with which Allah has distinguished man from woman is to resemble a woman too much. At the same time, we hope that the arguments we have mentioned will be enough for those who shave their beards. May Allah protect us from every act that He does not like or is not pleased with.

FEW ADVICE FOR HUSBAND AND WIFE.

While ending this book, I would like to offer some important advice for husband and wife.

1

Husband and wife should obey Allah Almighty, advise each other, and follow the rules of the Book and Sunnah. Do not prefer anything over the book Vasant for the sake of blind imitation, the customs of people, or your religion.

Allah Almighty said:

وَمَا كَانَ لِمُؤْمِنٍ وَلَا مُؤْمِنَةٍ إِذَا قَضَى ٱللَّهُ وَرَسُولُهُ أَمْرًا أَن يَكُونَ لَهُمُ ٱلْخِيَرَةُ مِنْ أَمْرِهِمْ وَمَن يَعْصِ ٱللَّهَ وَرَسُولَهُ فَقَدْ ضَلَّ ضَلَالًا مُّبِينًا

It is not open for a believing man or a believing woman, once Allah and His messenger have decided a thing, that they should have a choice about their matter; and whoever disobeys Allah and His messenger, he indeed gets off the track, falling into an open error.

2

Husband and wife should arrange each other's rights and duties, which are imposed on them by Allah Ta'ala.For example, a wife should not demand that she be given the same rights as her husband. On the basis of what Allah has given superiority to a man over a woman, he should not oppress her or beat her unjustly.

Allah Almighty said:

وَلَهُنَّ مِثْلُ الَّذِي عَلَيْهِنَّ بِالْمَعْرُوفِ وَلِلرِّجَالِ عَلَيْهِنَّ دَرَجَةٌ وَاللَّهُ عَزِيزٌ حَكِيمٌ

Women have rights similar to what they owe in recognized manner though for men there is a step above them. Allah is Mighty, Wise.

Allah Almighty said: (Translation)

Men are caretakers of women, since Allah has made some of them excel the others, and because of the wealth they have spent. So, the righteous women are obedient, (and) guard (the property and honor of their husbands) in (their) absence with the protection given by Allah. As for women of whom you fear rebellion, convince them, and leave them apart in beds, and beat

> them. Then, if they obey you, do not seek a way against them. Surely, Allah is the Highest, the Greatest.

Mu'awiyah bin Haydah (RA) asked the Prophet (PBUH): O Messenger of Allah (PBUH)! What right does wife have over one of us? The Prophet (peace and blessings of Allah be upon him) said: "When you eat yourself, eat it, and when you wear it yourself, wear it too. Do not curse his face, do not beat him, and keep him in the house (for punishment). Leave him alone.How do you like (beating the wife)? While you are related to each other (one soul and two bodies), but the beating that is permissible for them.

3

It is especially important for a woman to try to fulfill her husband's orders as much as possible. The reason for this is that Allah has given superiority to men over women.

As it has been mentioned in the previous verses;

Men dominate women.

Men are superior to women.

This position is also supported by numerous authentic hadiths.

In these hadiths, the conditions of a woman in both cases of obedience and disobedience to her husband have been described in detail. I feel it necessary to write down some of them so that the women of the present day may take advice from them.

Allah Almighty said:

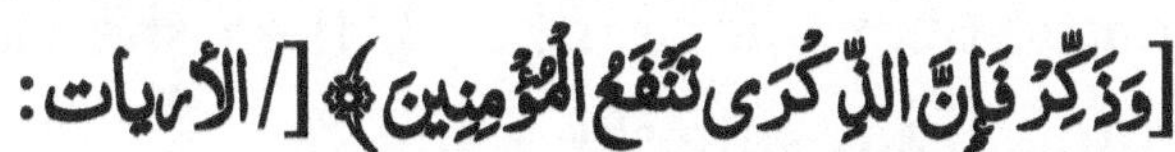

And keep reminding, because reminding benefits the believers.

First Hadith:

When the husband invites his wife to his bed and she refuses to come and the husband spends the night in a state of displeasure, then the angels continue to curse him until morning.

Second Hadith:

"By the One in Whose hand is the life of Muhammad, a woman cannot pay her dues to Allah until she pays her husband's dues." If he calls her and she is sitting on a camel's cradle, then do not restrain yourself from her (husband).

Third Hadith:

"When a woman prays the fivefold prayer, protects her private parts, obeys her husband, then she can enter heaven through any gate she wants."

It is clear from the previous Qur'an and Hadith that a man's service to a woman is necessary. This does not definitely prove that the husband cannot participate in this service. That is why Sayyida Ayesha Siddiqa (RA) says: The Prophet (PBUH) also used to help his family members.

At the end of this book, I pray to Allah Almighty to grant us the ability to understand the true religion and to follow it fully.

سُبْحَانَكَ اللَّهُمَّ وَبِحَمْدِكَ أَشْهَدُ أَنْ لَا إِلَهَ إِلَّا أَنْتَ اسْتَغْفِرُكَ وَأَتُوبُ إِلَيْكَ

Disclaimer:

Please note that if any spelling or typographical errors are identified within Etiquette of Intimacy in Islam, kindly bring them to our attention for correction. Your feedback is invaluable in ensuring the accuracy and quality of the content. Thank you for your understanding and assistance.

[ubaidqureshi0306@gmail.com]

Many Thanks!

We extend our heartfelt gratitude to all readers of **Etiquette of Intimacy in Islam**. Your interest in exploring the sacred principles of intimate relationships within the Islamic framework is deeply appreciated. Thank you for embarking on this journey with us and for your commitment to understanding and upholding the values of love, respect, and spirituality in marital life. Your support and engagement inspire us to continue sharing knowledge and wisdom on this important subject. Many thanks for being part of this meaningful endeavor.

Warm regards,

[Ibn-e-Anees]

[Author of Etiquette of Intimacy in Islam]

والحمد لله رب العٰلمين وصلَّى الله على خير خلقه محمد وأصحابه اجمعين

Did you love *Etiquette of Intimacy in Islam*? Then you should read *Easy Islam Birth to Death* by ibn-e-Anees!

A brief, extremely easy-to-learn book about Islam has been put together in response to this demand. It can be incorporated into the curricula of Islamic madrassas, schools, and elementary schools.

FAITH, PURITY, PRAYER (SALAH), EID PRAYER, SAJDAH TILAWA, TARAWEEH, FUNERAL PRAYER, FORTY SUNNAH PRAYERS(Dua's).

and other things have all been easily gathered. The trustworthy Hanafi legal treatises and Mishkwat Sharif's hadiths are the sources for the problems. As a final resort, after realizing the necessity, I composed forty duas based on Mishkwat Sharif and Hasan Hussain. It is intended that by incorporating this booklet into the curriculum, the madrasa and school administrators, as well as the responsible individuals within the schools, will get continued recognition and rewards.

Also by ibn-e-Anees

Halal Technique of Sacrifice (Qurbani) and Dua: A Comprehensive Guide for Eid al-Adha Rituals

Journey of a Lifetime: A Comprehensive Guide to Hajj and Umrah with Stunning Visuals

40 Rabbana Duas

First Murder on Earth: Life of Prophet Adam (AS)

99 Names of Allah and Attributes of the Divine

King of Wisdom: The Enchanting Tale of Prophet Sulaiman (PBUH)

Easy Islam Birth to Death

Etiquette of Intimacy in Islam